NATCHITOCHES HISTORIC DISTRICT WALKING TOUR
2020 EDITION

BRAD DISON

Copyright © 2020 Benjamin Brad Dison

Published By Harper Hill Publishing
Saline, Louisiana

Printed in the United States of America.

All rights reserved including the right of reproduction in whole or in part in any form.

ISBN: 9781706526391

CONTENTS

Introduction	5
In Case of Emergency	7
Calendar of Events	8
Weather	10
Walking Tour Maps	11
Walking Tour	13
Things To Do	95
Festivals	98
Eating	100
Shopping	103
Sleeping	110
About the Author	115
Notes	116

ACKNOWLEDGMENTS

I would like to express my sincere gratitude to Victoria Sheppard Dison, Jereme Dison, Kelly Sheppard, Julia Coleman, and Keith Vincent for their help throughout the writing and editing process.

Welcome to Natchitoches, the oldest permanent settlement in the Louisiana Purchase which included the states of Arkansas, Missouri, Iowa, Oklahoma, Kansas, Nebraska, South Dakota, as well as portions of Texas, Colorado, Wyoming, Montana, North Dakota, and Minnesota. Founded in 1714, Natchitoches predates New Orleans by four years.

Whether you are a lifelong resident of Natchitoches or just visiting, this book is sure to enrich your time in the Historic District. Emergency numbers, including police, fire, and hospital, are located in the first section of this book for easy access. Natchitoches' emergency services are always eager to help. There is always something fun going on in the Historic District. New events are added all the time, making it impossible to keep a calendar of events up to date in a printed book. The included calendar of events will give a good idea of what to expect. The weather in Natchitoches is hard to predict, but this book includes a chart showing the usual ranges of temperatures and rainfall.

Since you are on a self-guided walking tour, pick and choose which stops you want to make, and in which order you see them. The included maps and instructions should guide you through the walking tour with ease. Be sure to wear comfortable shoes and weather-appropriate clothing. This book includes many **REST STOPS** along the way. Take occasional breaks and enjoy the scenery.

The Historic District has a wide variety of food and drink that you are sure to enjoy including American, Italian, Cajun, Creole, seafood, steak, candy, snacks, and even Japanese Sushi. Like my mother always said, "If you go hungry, it's your own fault."

One of the most impressive things about the Historic District is that you can sleep in many of the historic homes. Most of us rarely get the opportunity to sleep in a fully restored two hundred year old home. With each stay, you become part of the home's history, and a part of Natchitoches' history.

IN CASE OF EMERGENCY

Natchitoches Regional Medical Center
(318) 214-4200
501 Keyser Avenue

Natchitoches Police Department
(318) 352-8101
400 Amulet Street

Natchitoches Parish Sheriff's Department
(318) 352-6432
200 Church Street

Natchitoches Fire Department
(318) 357-3860
700 E. Second Street

HISTORIC DISTRICT CALENDAR OF EVENTS

There is always something fun going on in the Historic District. New events are added all the time and event dates can change, making it impossible to keep a calendar of events up to date in a printed book. The included calendar of events will give a good idea of what to expect.

JANUARY
- Festival of Lights (November through the first week of January)

FEBRUARY
- Krewe of Dionysos Mardi Gras Parade

MARCH
- Art Along the Bricks
- Bloomin' on the Bricks
- Cane River Film Festival
- Encampment at Fort St. Jean Baptiste

APRIL
- Cane River Green Market
- Natchitoches Jazz and R&B Festival

MAY
- Sale on the Trail

JUNE
- Cane River Green Market
- Louisiana Sports Hall of Fame Induction Weekend

JULY
- Cane River Green Market
- Celebration on the Cane/Fourth of July Celebration

AUGUST
- Back to School Bash

SEPTEMBER
- Boogie on the Bricks (after NSU home football game)
- Cane River Zydeco Festival
- Meat Pie Festival

OCTOBER
- Boogie on the Bricks (after NSU home football game)
- Cane River Green Market's Harvest Celebration
- Creole Heritage Celebration
- Fall Tour of Homes
- Historic Cemetery Tour
- Witch Way to Main Street

NOVEMBER
- Boogie on the Bricks (after NSU home football game)
- Festival of Lights Kickoff
- Holiday Open House

DECEMBER
- Christmas by Candlelight Tour of Homes
- Christmas Downriver
- Encampment at Fort St. Jean Baptiste
- Festival of Lights
- Natchitoches Christmas Festival

For more up-to-date information, search online for the name of the event you wish to experience and be sure to include the word Natchitoches in your search.

WEATHER

	Avg. Min. Temp.	Avg. Max. Temp.	Avg. Rainfall
JANUARY	36°F	57°F	5.67 inches
FEBRUARY	39°F	62°F	4.41 inches
MARCH	46°F	70°F	5.35 inches
APRIL	53°F	77°F	4.53 inches
MAY	62°F	84°F	5.83 inches
JUNE	70°F	90°F	4.49 inches
JULY	74°F	93°F	3.39 inches
AUGUST	73°F	93°F	3.50 inches
SEPTEMBER	66°F	88°F	3.07 inches
OCTOBER	54°F	79°F	4.13 inches
NOVEMBER	45°F	68°F	4.61 inches
DECEMBER	38°F	59°F	5.91 inches

The weather in Natchitoches is generally humid. If you visit in the summer months, dress appropriately. Bring bottles of water, sunblock, sunshades, a hat or umbrella for shade, and something to fan yourself with. If you visit in the winter months, bring a jacket, gloves, ear muffs, and maybe a scarf.

NATCHITOCHES HISTORIC DISTRICT WALKING TOUR

MAPS

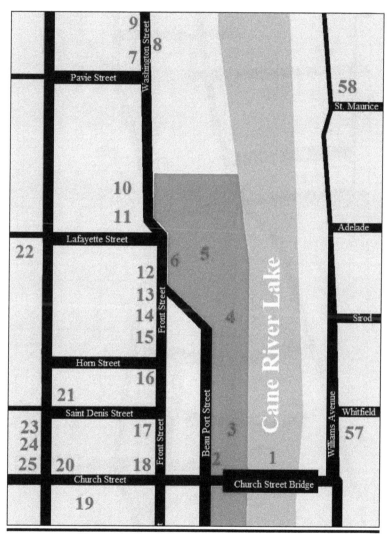

Figure 1. North Portion of Walking Tour

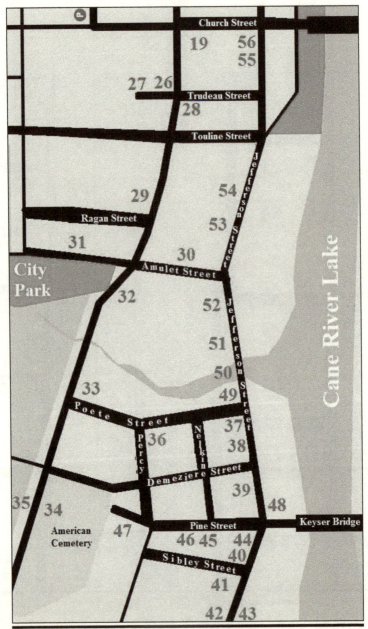

Figure 2. South Portion of Walking Tour

HISTORIC DISTRICT WALKING TOUR

1. CANE RIVER LAKE

- *START HALFWAY ACROSS CHURCH STREET BRIDGE AND LOOK UPSTREAM (AWAY FROM THE FOUNTAIN).*

Cane River Lake is a thirty-five-mile-long lake which was once a part of Red River. In 1714, Louisiana Governor Antoine Laumet de la Mothe, sieur de Cadillac, sent French Canadian explorer Louis Juchereau de St. Denis and a group of men on an expedition on this river to meet and trade with the Natchitoches Indians.[1] The name Natchitoches translates to "chinquapin eaters," a type of nut similar to a chestnut.[2] Their village was at the upper end of the navigable part of the river. Because of this expedition, St. Denis has been given credit for founding the city of Natchitoches.[3]

Riverboats once travelled back and forth between New Orleans and Natchitoches when the water was high enough to deliver goods and passengers, which was usually only between the months of January and June.[4] Riverboats could only go a little further upstream from this spot because the river was blocked by the Great Raft, a series of driftwood log jams that blocked about 160 miles of Red River north of Natchitoches.[5] By 1838, workers led by Henry Miller Shreve had cleared the log jam from Red River, but a second log jam gradually blocked the river again. In 1873, workers led by Eugene Woodruff cleared the second log jam and opened river travel from Shreveport to New Orleans.

For months at a time, Red River in Natchitoches was little more than a trickle of water. In 1916, the Natchitoches Parish Police Jury voted and passed a resolution to dam the 35-mile section, and to recognize it as a "public highway."[6] That same year, workers dammed Cane River by placing bales of hay where Cane River connected to Red River. This created Cane River Lake. The Police Jury created the lake to be used "extensively by planters residing at Bermuda, Melrose, and adjacent villages, for shipping their produce to Natchitoches." In March, 1917, J.H. Henry of Melrose was the first person to use Cane River Lake for its new purpose when he shipped a barge containing "ten of the largest wagons" filled with hay to Natchitoches.[7]

Cane River Lake quickly became a sportsman's paradise. In October, 1917, "P.C. Rogers received 8,800 fish from the government," and stocked the lake with a variety of fish including "trout, white perch, bream, goggle-eyed perch, and rock bass."[8] Duck season that year turned out to be popular for hunters as it "brought out as many hunters as ducks." Several duck hunters received fines for shooting their guns on the lake inside the city limits.[9]

- *Walk back to Front Street and turn right and you will see...*

2. BRICK ROAD AND FRONT STREET CHAIRS

Before 1904, all of the streets in Natchitoches were dirt. Travel in the city was dusty in dry weather and muddy in wet weather. In 1904, workers laid bricks over the dirt road for better and cleaner transportation. The brick road worked perfectly for horse-drawn buggies but not as well once automobiles became the transportation of choice. Over the years of automobile traffic, the brick road became rough and bumpy.[10] Many locals avoided driving on Front Street altogether. In 1958, a group of local businessmen requested that the State Highway Department "cover the brick pavement with an overlay of blacktop." The Association of Women for the preservation of Historic Natchitoches fought back.[11] Women from the association saved the brick road by laying arm-in-arm in front of the Highway Department's heavy machinery.

In March, 2008, workers began to rehabilitate Front Street and carefully removed, catalogued, and stacked each brick.[12] Three months later, workers unearthed artifacts underneath the bricks including Indian pottery, shells, a

1900 silver dollar, and a bottle of "soothing cream" from the mid-1800s, which was used to comfort babies when they were teething. They also uncovered building foundations including one dating from the 1700s. Work on the project slowed while Archaeologists studied the artifacts. They photographed each artifact and replaced them where they were found.[13] They laid a new foundation and replaced each brick by hand. In November, 2008, workers completed the rehabilitation project which restored the historic brick road.[14] If you look closely at the wrought iron chairs on the Riverbank you will see the names of prominent citizens and businesses in the ironwork.

- *Take the stairs down to the Riverbank. If necessary, a wheelchair ramp is just a short distance further.*

3. THE RIVERBANK
Front Street

The Riverbank is the focal point for almost all outdoor events held in Natchitoches. There is something happening on the Riverbank nearly every weekend whether it be festivals, bands performing, farmer's markets, car shows, or firework displays, but the largest of all is the Christmas Festival. On Christmas Festival day, tens of thousands of people gather on the Riverbank and Front Street to listen to music, eat good food, and watch a firework and laser show set to music. In 2017, the City totally renovated the Riverbank. Bathrooms are located at the south end of the Riverbank. To get to them, walk south along Cane River Lake. (Cane River Lake will be on your left).

- *Walk North along Cane River Lake until you get to the Roque House. (Cane River Lake will be on your right.)*

4. THE ROQUE HOUSE

This is one of about five unaltered pure colonial French dwellings left in Louisiana.[15] In August, 1967, workers moved the fifty-five-ton Roque House to its current location from the Melrose area, twenty miles down Cane River Lake, and began the rigorous restoration process.[16] The house is named after Madame Aubin Roque, the last person to live in the house.[17] It was built in the late 1700s or very early 1800s by fitting hand-hewn cypress beams together and filling in the voids with "bousillage," a mixture of clay and fibrous materials such as deer hair and Spanish moss.[18] Once dry, bousillage is basically a single large brick. If you look closely you can see the axe marks in the cypress beams.

- *Walk to the other side of the Roque House and you will enter Beau Jardin.*

5. BEAU JARDIN

Beau Jardin, French for beautiful garden, is considered to be one of the most romantic and peaceful places in the Historic District. This is a favorite spot for picnics, photos, proposals, outdoor weddings, receptions, and renewing your vows. This tranquil park is the perfect place to relax. Take a few minutes to enjoy the sound of the water cascading down the waterfall, and watch the stream pass beneath your feet as you stand on the arched wooden bridge.

- *This is a good **REST STOP**.*
- *Walk up the 31 steps and turn left and you will see...*

6. BUST OF LOUIS JUCHEREAU DE ST. DENIS

St. Denis (Saint Duh-nee) is considered the founder of Natchitoches, the oldest permanent settlement in the Louisiana Purchase. In 1714, he travelled to this area to trade with the Natchitoches Indians. Within a few years he and his men built Fort St. Jean Baptiste on the river as a trading post and for self-protection. In 1985, sculptor Larry Crowder cast this bust in bronze, and city leaders placed it near the end of the El Camino Real. The El Camino Real, Spanish for the King's Highway, was a trading route connecting Natchitoches, to Nacogdoches, TX, San Antonio, TX, and ending at Mexico City.

- ***Restrooms** are located on the other side of the stairs to Beau Jardin.*
- *The flower garden in the center of the brick road is a popular spot for pictures.*
- *Walk past Maglieaux's Restaurant until you see on the left...*

7. MAGNOLIAS HOUSE
902 Washington Street

The Magnolias House was built in about 1805, in the Greek Revival style. Many of the windows in this house are original. You can easily spot the originals from a distance by looking for waviness in the glass. Pick out a widow and stare at it while moving your head left and right. Modern windows will be perfectly smooth and will not have the waviness effect. A local legend claims that General James Wilkinson was living here in July, 1806, when he received a coded message from former Vice President of the United States, Aaron Burr.[19] (This being the same Aaron Burr who, two years earlier, famously killed Alexander Hamilton in a duel. The duel ended Burr's political career and he moved to northeast Louisiana.) Burr's letter detailed his plans to create a new country in the middle of North America. General Wilkinson informed President Thomas Jefferson of the Burr Conspiracy, but Jefferson, like many other politicians in Washington, thought Wilkinson was part of the conspiracy. Burr was arrested, tried, and found not guilty. Following the Burr Conspiracy, General Wilkinson was investigated twice by Congress, but not charged with any crime.

- *A few houses up on the right you will see...*

8. VIOLET HILL BED & BREAKFAST
917 Washington Street

When this building was built in 1891, it looked much different than it does today. It originally had just four rooms, and housed the Natchitoches Ice Company, the first ice company in town.[20] Within a month of completion, the Natchitoches Ice Company produced three tons of ice each day.[21] In 1904, Dr. Edward Lawton bought the building and used it as his office, called the Cottage Sanatorium. Three years later he began adding rooms to the structure and used it as his family home.[22] Violet Hill now operates as a bed and breakfast.

- *Across the road you will see...*

9. SWEET CANE INN
926 Washington Street

Built for Congressman Phanor Breazeale in the late 1800s, this Victorian home now known as the Sweet Cane Inn boasts 11 fireplaces, 12-foot ceilings, stained glass windows, and multiple balconies. President William Howard Taft once spent the night here.[23]

Phanor Breazeale's career started as a clerk in a Natchitoches mercantile establishment. He studied to become an attorney and acted as a clerk of the Louisiana Supreme Court in New Orleans. After graduating from Tulane University's law department in 1881, he began practicing law in Natchitoches. In 1888, he was elected to the Natchitoches Parish Police Jury, his first elected position. He was district attorney from 1892 to 1900, a member of the State Constitutional Convention in 1898 and 1921, and a member of the national House of Representatives from 1899 to 1905. He returned to Natchitoches to practice law. In 1908, Phanor Breazeale was appointed as a member of the commission to codify the criminal laws of Louisiana and to prepare a code of criminal procedure. He was a delegate to the Democratic National Convention in 1908 and again in 1916. The Shreveport Times claimed that his public career was "among the most distinguished of any figure in the state."[24]

For decades, residents and visitors have claimed that the house is haunted. One visitor from Florida said he lost a pair of prescription glasses during his stay in Natchitoches. He searched but was unable to find his glasses. While getting ready for bed he piled his dirty clothes on the floor next to his bed. When he awoke the next morning, his laundry had been neatly folded and his lost glasses sat on top of the laundry. A young girl staying in the house heard a noise one night near one of the many windows. She quickly took a flash photo of the window. The picture showed her reflection with a short black woman with a bun hairdo standing behind her. None of the registered guests fit that description. Several visitors have described seeing this woman.[25] Previous owners described a rain shower one night in the house but searches revealed no leaking pipes. Doors, including large, heavy pocket doors, sometimes open and close without explanation.[26]

- *Cross the street and head back the direction from which you came (toward the brick road). The Bank of Montgomery Courtyard on the right is a nice place for a **REST STOP**.*
- *Continue walking back to the brick road until you see on the right...*

10. SOMPAYRAC BUILDING/PIONEER PUB
812 Washington Street

The Sompayrac Building was built in 1840 and used as a bank for many years. The building was renovated to the style you see here just before World War II. The building is named after Ambroise Sompayrac, "an early French settler who became a prominent planter, importer, and banker in the area."[27] Today, the Pioneer Pub occupies the building. Here, you can get a mouth-watering appetizer called "The Wookie."[28]

- *Next door you will see...*

11. LOUISIANA SPORTS HALL OF FAME AND NORTHWEST LOUISIANA HISTORY MUSEUM
500 Front Street

The exterior of the Louisiana Sports Hall of Fame is in direct contrast to the other buildings in the Historic District. Whereas most of the buildings in the Historic District are examples of architecture from the past, the modern design of the Louisiana Sports Hall of Fame seems to be from the future. Exhibits include race cars, team jerseys, balls, trophies, and anything else you can think of relating to sports. In addition to sports, their collection includes paintings by internationally renowned folk artist Clementine Hunter, artifacts from an old gas station, items relating to the sawmill industry, and much more. For more information on entrance fees and hours, please see the Things To Do in the Historic District section.

- *Restrooms* are just inside the door to the right.
- Cross the street near the Cypress trees and walk along Front Street until you see…

12. KAFFIE-FREDERICK GENERAL MERCANTILE
758 Front Street

Walking into Kaffie-Frederick's General Mercantile is the closest we can come to going back in time. In 1863, in the midst of the Civil War, two Jewish immigrants, the Kaffie brothers, began a door-to-door sales operation in Natchitoches. The Kaffie brothers prospered and built this building in 1893. Titus Frederick worked for the Kaffie brothers and worked his way up until he became general manager. After World War II, Titus Frederick bought the store, and it has remained in the Frederick family ever since.

In some ways, this store is like a museum, but it is a functioning store specializing in home, kitchen, garden, hardware, children's items, and just about anything else you can think of. Employees still use the original freight elevator, although it is now electrically powered. Make a purchase and an employee will "ring you up" on the original hand-crank cash register that the Kaffie brothers bought in 1917.[29] If you look closely throughout the store you will see vintage original photographs of the store. Notice the large skylight in the center of the ceiling. The Kaffie brothers built the store before modern lighting became popular. They used many windows and skylights for natural lighting because it was effective in the daylight hours and less expensive than using oil lamps. In 1897, $1.00 would get your choice of the following items; a nice water cooler, 20 pounds of sugar, 8 pounds of "good" coffee, 30 bars of soap, or 5 pounds of Battle Ax tobacco.[30]

- *Next door you will see...*

13. DUCOURNAU BUILDING
750 Front Street

In about 1835, businessman Francois LaFonte built this two-and-a-half story building with the store on the first floor and a townhouse above. This building is a rare example of French Creole mercantile architecture. The 10-foot wide brick opening on the right side of the building was a carriageway which leads to a rear brick courtyard known as Ducournau Square. Carriages delivered goods to the stores on the bottom floor through this carriageway. You can almost hear the clip clop of horses passing through the carriageway. The entrance to the townhouse is located in Ducournau Square, at the back of the building. The front and rear of the building has iron-laced second floor galleries. Ducournau Building is named for J.A. Ducournau, a local merchant who purchased the building in 1881. Today, the townhouse is a bed and breakfast.[31] The first floor houses the Hana Japanese Sushi Bar and Grill.

- *Next door you will see...*

14. BLANCHARD BUILDING
740 Front Street

In 1853, Gabriel Prudhomme chartered a ship from Europe to transport the building materials for this structure. It was originally owned by Gustave "Gus" Lacoste and called the Lacoste Building.[32] In the late 1800s, the bottom floor of the Lacoste Building housed a dry goods store and a saloon with three billiard tables.[33] Caspari & Dietrick's store sold dry goods, clothing, hats, boots, shoes, groceries, crockery, and hardware, all of which were sold "at less than New Orleans prices."[34] Attorney William Levy had his law office upstairs.[35] Carriages delivered merchandise through the central carriageway to the rear of the stores.[36] It was eventually renamed the Blanchard Building.[37] This is one of the most lavishly wrought iron-decorated buildings in the Historic District.

- *Next door you will see...*

15. HUGHES BUILDING
700 Front Street

Built in 1853 by architect Gabriel Prudhomme, the Hughes Building housed several types of businesses in the 1800s. For a while, it was the Hughes and Aaron Saloon and Billiard hall, where on Sunday nights white-coated waiters served turkey suppers by candlelight. It was elaborately decorated and was a sort of gentleman's club. Parker's Shoe Store once occupied the first floor of the north half of the building. In 1900, the Hughes Dry Goods store occupied the first floor. Beginning in 1959, the second floor housed the radio station KNOC, which expanded in 1965 to include radio station KDBH, Natchitoches' first FM radio station.[38] In 1973, fire gutted the dry goods store but the radio station was unharmed. Today, shops occupy the first floor as they have for the last 150 years. If you look at the threshold at the entrance to the store you can still see the name of the building written in tiles. Like the Ducournau Building, the front and rear of the Hughes Building have iron-laced second floor galleries. Walk around to the back of the building to see the imported French staircase.

- *Walk to the corner of Horn Street and Front Street.*

16. CHRISTMAS DAY SHOOTOUT
Corner of Front Street and Horn Street

At about 9 am on Christmas morning, 1875, thirty-three-year-old Edward L. Pierson, a young lawyer in Natchitoches and a State Representative, and thirty-two-year-old James H. Cosgrove, editor of the Natchitoches *People's Vindicator*, got into a heated argument at the corner of Horn Street and Front Street.[39] The feud began when Cosgrove printed scathing articles about Pierson in the *People's Vindicator*. Cosgrove's articles claimed that Pierson had deserted the Confederate ranks during the Civil War on several occasions. He claimed Pierson had been sentenced to death twice for deserting, but escaped before either sentence could be carried out. In short, Cosgrove challenged Pierson's honor. Cosgrove claimed Pierson challenged him to a duel but Cosgrove did not accept the challenge because he "could not afford Pierson the satisfaction due a gentleman."[40]

Eyewitness accounts vary greatly on exactly how the fight began on Christmas morning, what kinds of weapons were used, and locations of injuries. What sources agree upon is that Cosgrove shot Pierson. Pierson ran to St. Denis Street, turned right and ran toward Second Street, all the while being chased by Cosgrove. Pierson ran toward his house on Second Street when Cosgrove shot him multiple times. Pierson made it to the gateway of his house and his youngest sister helped him inside. Within thirty minutes, Pierson died from his wounds. Witnesses said a blood trail ran the complete path Pierson took beginning at this intersection to his front door on Second Street. Edward L. Pierson was buried in the American Cemetery which we will see later on the tour.[41]

- *Walk to the corner of Front Street and St. Denis Street.*

17. CRAZY CROPPER AND THE MAYOR
Corner of Front Street and St. Denis Street

Near this spot at noon on November 11, 1922, E.S. Cropper had a confrontation with Natchitoches Mayor Theodore Edward Poleman. Cropper earned money by selling water from a mineral well located on his property. The city made street improvements near his property and, after a brief period, the well caved in. Cropper claimed that the cave-in was due to the street improvements, but an investigation showed that the damage was due to an overflow.[42] Although Mayor Poleman's investigative committee found that the city was not to blame, the individual committee members personally donated money to fix the well. Cropper was unhappy with this solution because, he argued, his customers had begun buying their water from another source. Cropper held Mayor Poleman personally responsible and threatened to kill him on several occasions. Mayor Poleman said that unless he could settle the dispute with Cropper, he would resign because the "threats kept him continually in suspense." At noon, November 11,

1922, E.S. Cropper shot Mayor Poleman twice. One bullet passed through his liver and the other struck him in the hip.[43] When police arrived, Cropper still held the smoking gun in his hand and had another .38 revolver in his pocket. Mayor Poleman never regained consciousness. He developed pneumonia and died at his home on the night of November 14, 1922.[44] He is buried in the American Cemetery, which we will see later on the tour. During the trial, jurors learned that since childhood E.S. Cropper was known as Crazy Cropper. He claimed an angel appeared to him one night and showed him where to dig the "wonder well." Crazy Cropper was found guilty of murder and was sentenced to life imprisonment.[45] A year later, Crazy Cropper was transferred to the Jackson Insane Asylum where he lived for the remainder of his life.[46]

- *Walk to the corner of Front Street and Church Street.*

18. SITE OF CHURCH OF ST. FRANCIS & TOMB OF ST. DENIS
Corner of Front Street and Church Street

In the early months of 1720, citizens of Natchitoches built the church of St. Francis, the first Catholic Church in Natchitoches, on this spot facing away from Front Street. It was a simple structure made of hand hewn logs. In 1744, Louis Juchereau de St. Denis, founder of Natchitoches, died and, some historians argue, was buried either beneath the floor of the church or in the churchyard surrounding the structure.[47] Some historians argue that the first Catholic Church was built at Fort St. Jean Baptiste, meaning St. Denis is buried there. Other historians argue that St. Denis is buried in the American Cemetery.[48] Sometime after St. Denis' death, the church was destroyed by fire but was quickly rebuilt. In March, 1838, another fire destroyed the second church of St. Francis. This fire started in the kitchen of Ms. Crossman, who lived on Second Street. The fire quickly spread and consumed the church, a law office, and four homes.[49] It was replaced by the Church of the

Immaculate Conception, built on the same block but facing Second Street. We will visit this church later on the tour. In 1934, the Daughters of the American Revolution presented the historical marker located on the corner of the current building which claims that the tomb is under this building.[50]

- *Take a quick look at the second floor of the building across the street. Construction workers renovating this building removed several layers of plaster and paint and found these original decorative iron fleurs de lis.*
- *From Front Street, turn right on Church Street, walk about half a block and look to your left to see...*

19. RECTORY & BISHOP'S HOUSE
Church Street

In 1885, the Catholic Rectory was built in New Orleans. It was dismantled and shipped to Natchitoches on a steamboat and reassembled. It is said to be the first prefabricated building in the state.[51] In 1855, the Old Seminary was built to house and teach seminary students. The Bishop Martin Museum houses early church records dating back to 1724 and other church artifacts.[52] The museum is named after Bishop Augustus Marie Aloysius Martin. Bishop Martin was born in France in 1803 and became a priest twenty-five years later. In 1853, he became the first Bishop of Natchitoches. Bishop Martin died in 1875, and is buried near the altar in the Minor Basilica of Immaculate Conception, our next stop.[53]

- *Walk to the corner of Church Street and Second Street, then turn right...*

20. MINOR BASILICA OF IMMACULATE CONCEPTION
145 Church Street

In 1856, parishioners built this church to replace the one destroyed by fire. It has been renovated twice, once in 1955 and again in 1996. Parishioners raised the majority of the $1.2 million needed to renovate the church back to its 1892 appearance. The church was previously air conditioned but, until the renovations, overhead duct work took away from its grandeur. Construction workers took steps to ensure that all signs of modernization, including the duct work, were hidden from view. With the exception of the pews, all of the interior furnishings, including the four French crystal chandeliers suspended from the ceiling, were imported from France.[54] In 2009, Pope Benedict XVI designated the Immaculate Conception Church a Minor Basilica for its rare historical significance.[55] Look to the left of the front doors and you will see the grave of Reverend Anthony Piegay, French-born Vicar General who was assistant and pastor of Immaculate Conception Church until his death in 1939. Step inside and take a look at the spiral staircase and notice that it has no center support. Group tours are available by appointment at 318-352-3422.

- *Walk one block north along Second Street (the Church will be on your right) and look at the sidewalk in front of City Bank and Trust Company to see...*

21. NATCHITOCHES WALK OF FAME

Look for several fleurs de lis in the sidewalk containing the names of people who have made a significant contribution to Natchitoches through entertainment, sports, the arts and cultural activities. Several movies have been filmed in Natchitoches including the 1959 Western entitled *The Horse Soldiers,* starring John Wayne and William Holden, and the 1989 comedy-drama entitled *Steel Magnolias,* starring Sally Field, Dolly Parton, Shirley MacLaine, Daryl Hannah, Olympia Dukakis, and Julia Roberts. Look for their names and others in the fleurs de lis.

- *Walk one block north along Second Street, cross the street near the entrance to the Chateau Saint Denis. Look for a historical marker entitled...*

22. SITE OF FORT CLAIBORNE
750 Second Street

The Natchitoches Events Center is the site of Fort Claiborne, which was the first United States fort constructed after the Louisiana Purchase.[56] It was built in 1805 to replace Fort St. Jean Baptiste. From the late-1700s to the mid-1800s, Natchitoches was the boundary between Spanish Texas and French Louisiana. The Spanish continually challenged the border. About two hundred men were garrisoned at Fort Claiborne.[57] In the spring of 1806, the Spanish government ordered a military corps from Texas toward Natchitoches to reclaim what Spanish Governor Simón de Herrera claimed was the ancient boundary of the Province of Texas. United States President Thomas Jefferson put General James Wilkinson in command of the small force assembled at Natchitoches. General Wilkinson "found them unprepared," but, as soon as they were equipped and prepared for action, he advanced against the Spanish at Los Adias. Spain and the United States agreed upon the Neutral Strip agreement, which made the disputed territory a no man's land.[58] In 1821, Spain surrendered any claim to the no man's land to the United States. The following year, Fort Claiborne was abandoned and was replaced by Fort Jesup, 31 miles southwest of Natchitoches.[59]

- *Walk back toward Church Street (the Events Center will be on your right) until you come to...*

23. LASYONE'S MEAT PIE KITCHEN
622 Second Street

For twenty-five years, James Lasyone worked in a grocery store next door to this site. While working there, he began experimenting with different ingredients to perfect the meat pie, a product which peddlers once sold from carts on Front Street. After two years of experimenting, his meat pie recipe was ready for the masses. In about 1967, with $6.96 and a single iron pot, he opened a five-by-nine foot restaurant in this building. When other businesses in the building closed, Lasyone leased and modified the space, and increased the size of the restaurant and his menu. Within a short time, Lasyone's restaurant took up the whole bottom floor. The second floor was leased to the Masonic Lodge. With no further room to expand, Lasyone considered moving to another location. However, the owner eventually put the whole building up for sale and Lasyone bought it. In the mid-1980s, when the average order ranged from between ten to fifteen dozen meat pies, Lasyone received an order unlike any other. A customer in

Shreveport ordered 20,000 meat pies. It took Lasyone four months, but he filled the order.[60] James Lasyone died in 2015, and his two daughters now run the restaurant.[61]

- *Next to Lasyone's you will see a...*

24. VETERANS AND MEMORIAL PARK

Officially dedicated on Veteran's Day, November 11, 2014, this park honors the men and women who have served or are serving in the military. Take a few minutes to look around at the curved monument and fountain. Notice the brick walkway in the park which lists the names, rank, and other information of locals who have served in various branches of the military.

- *This is a good **REST STOP**.*
- *The large red brick building beside you is...*

(Courtesy of Keith Vincent.)

25. OLD COURTHOUSE
600 Second Street

In 1896, the Favrot and Livaudais architectural firm of New Orleans built this courthouse in the Richardsonian Romanesque style. The center tower and the arched, recessed windows are typical of that style. In 1933, a fire damaged the building and it was renovated. The roofline over the stairwell and the tower were lowered. Compare the picture above to the Old Courthouse and you will notice several differences. Legends persist that criminals who were sentenced to death were marched up the spiral staircase in the tower and were hung near the windows of the courthouse in view of the public. In reality, when someone was sentenced to death in Natchitoches Parish, carpenters built gallows behind the courthouse and did not hang them in the tower. For example, on April 24, 1904, Henry Johnson and his wife got into an argument, which escalated into Henry beating his wife. Henry's half-brother, Lewis Richards, tried to intervene. This further enraged Johnson who shot Richards twice with a shotgun, killing him instantly.[62] Henry was convicted for the murder and sentenced to death. Newspapers reported that carpenters built the gallows for the hanging.[63] On September 23, 1904, Henry Johnson was legally hanged at the courthouse for killing his half-brother, Lewis Richards.[64] No records could be found which showed that hangings took place in the tower. In 1940, with the completion of the new courthouse, the old courthouse became obsolete. The Old Courthouse currently houses the Natchitoches Genealogy Library.

- *Cross the street and walk past the fire station until you reach the corner of Second Street and Trudeau Street.*

26. CUNNINGHAM LAW OFFICE BUILDING
550 Second Street

In 1860, Attorney Henry Safford paid the strange sum of $1,883.44 5/12 (that is 5/12 of a cent) to have this structure built. Carpenters built it with thirty-six-foot virgin pine sills held together with wooden pegs. They are still as strong today as they were when completed. This building has housed eight generations of attorneys. It is named after the Cunningham family. In 1988, after one hundred twenty eight years as a law office, it closed.[65] Six years later, the Natchitoches Historic Foundation purchased and restored the Cunningham Law Office Building.[66] The building has rare twin chimneys in the center of the building for heating each side of the duplex office.

- *Walk behind the Cunningham Law Office Building to find...*

27. MILDRED BAILEY PARK (REST STOP)
Behind 550 Second Street

Dr. Mildred Bailey was born on March 29, 1926, in Natchitoches. She was a teacher and Dean of Graduate Studies and Research at Northwestern State University in Natchitoches. She was a founding member of the Natchitoches Historic Foundation. She purchased and restored the Chaplin House in Natchitoches. Bailey was an admirer of Clementine Hunter's paintings and the two became friends. She recorded at least twenty-two oral histories on Clementine Hunter's life and art. She spent most of her life in the pursuit of preserving the history of Natchitoches.

- *This is a good **REST STOP**.*
- *Diagonally across the street from the Cunningham Law Office Building you will see...*

28. TRINITY EPISCOPAL CHURCH
533 Second Street

On Sunday, March 31, 1839, Reverend Leonidas Polk, for whom Fort Polk in Leesville was named, led the first Episcopal service in Natchitoches in the courthouse.[67] (Leonidas Polk became known as "the fighting Bishop" of the Confederacy during the Civil War.)[68] In 1843, the congregation converted an old store building into a church. In 1855 the congregation purchased the land and, three years later, workers completed the Trinity Episcopal Church. On Ash Wednesday, 1858, the congregation held the first service in the church although only the walls, floor, and ceiling were completed. It was the first non-Catholic church built in Natchitoches and only the third Episcopal Church in Louisiana. The exterior walls vary in thickness from twenty-two to twenty-eight inches. The Troy Bell Foundry in Troy, New York, cast the bell especially for this church. It is said to be made of one-third silver. Inside you will see large laminated wooden arches which span the width of the building. The floors are made of hand-hewn lumber.[69] This was Truvy's church and the location of the funeral in *Steel Magnolias*.

- *Just down the block on the right you will see...*

29. CHAPLIN HOUSE
434 Second Street

In 1892, Thomas Percy Chaplin had this house built for his wife Marie Lisa Breazeale. Some of the walls inside the Chaplin House have hand-printed wallpaper, one of which was designed by William Morris, who created wallpapers and fabrics for Queen Victoria. Most of the furniture is original to the house and belonged to the Chaplin family. In 1978, Dr. Mildred Bailey (we just visited a park named in her honor) purchased and restored the Chaplin House.[70] This was Aunt Fern's home in *Steel Magnolias*.

- *Walk to the next street, Amulet Street, and turn left until you see...*

30. CHAMARD-DUNAHOE HOUSE
120 Amulet Street

In about 1760, soldiers, Native Americans, and slaves built the Chamard-Dunahoe House in the French-Colonial style. In 1768, Andre Chamard purchased the house from Commandant Caesar Borme of Fort St. Jean Baptiste. Chamard was a French descendant of the Bourbon family of France. In 1873, a little over a hundred years later, Colonel William H. Jack bought the home for $5,000.00. Colonel Jack loved exotic birds and his backyard held his collection which included peacocks, eagles, and pheasants.[71]

- *Walk back towards Second Street. Cross it and continue along Amulet Street until you see...*

31. TEXAS & PACIFIC RAILWAY DEPOT
314 Amulet Street

In 1900, this railroad depot, the first in Natchitoches, enabled passengers and freight to travel southeast to New Orleans and northwest to Shreveport. The rail line continued on to El Paso, Texas, and toward the Pacific Ocean.[72] This building served as the depot until June, 1927, when a larger depot was built a few blocks away.[73] The building was restored in 1979 and is used for the Natchitoches City Court.

- *Across the street is the City Park. This is a good **REST STOP**.*
- *Walk back to Second Street and turn right until you see...*

32. MASON SALTER FURNITURE STORE
365 Second Street

In 1939, an enthusiastic thirty-year-old Mason Salter rented a twenty foot by fifty foot building on Second Street and opened a furniture store. Sales were strong until the United States entered World War II two years later, and manufacturing plants retooled for the war effort. Undeterred, when the war ended in 1944, he bought land and built this 10,000 square foot store. Knowing he would need storage space, Mason had the building built with a 3,000 square foot basement. Soldiers returning home from the war built new houses in record numbers. These new houses needed furnishing and the furniture store prospered. Mason added two more warehouses, and increased the size of the showroom space to 14,000 square feet. Today, Mason's son and daughter-in-law continue to operate the furniture store with the same vision and spirit as the thirty-year-old enthusiastic Mason Salter.[74]

- *Continue walking along Second Street until you see...*

33. JUDGE PORTER HOUSE
321 Second Street

In 1912, Thomas F. Porter, Sr. carefully dismantled an existing home near this location and used the lumber to construct this home. The house took only three months to build at a total cost $1,500.00. The 32,000 square-foot Judge Porter House has an eight-columned, two-story gallery, five fireplaces, and has fifteen windows over eight feet in height. These windows were originally used as doorways to the gallery.[75] The house is named after its builder, Thomas F. Porter, Sr., but he was not an actual judge. Thomas Sr. was a farmer.[76] It is likely that the house was mistakenly named after his son, Thomas F. Porter, Jr. who, in 1906, graduated with honors from Yale Law School,[77] and by 1922 was a judge in Lake Charles, Louisiana.[78]

- *Continue walking along Second Street for about a block until you see on your left...*

34. AMERICAN CEMETERY
Across from 212 Second Street

The American Cemetery is one of the oldest remaining cemeteries in the United States. No one really knows how many people are buried here because some of the bodies are buried three and four deep. All creeds and colors are buried here including, but not limited to, Spanish, French, Native American, and, of course, Americans. Locals see the cemetery as a holy place but do not fear it. In the 1930s, newspapers noted that locals used it as a "short cut" or "blind alley" to get to their destination, and on summer's evenings "students study and lovers court." [79]

American Cemetery is the location of the second Fort St. Jean Baptiste which was built in 1721. The first was built in 1715 on an island in what is now Cane River Lake but was rebuilt here due to constant flooding.[80] In 1884,[81] 1889,[82] and 1939, newspapers reported that the remains of the fort were still visible in the cemetery,[83] and could "be located easily."[84] In 1889, Mr. Will H. Tunnard reported that "the remains of the bastions, ramparts and trenches of this fortress... are still plainly traceable."[85] The dead were buried inside the walls of the fort and, as time passed and more people died, the burials expanded to include the area surrounding the fort.[86]

In 1836, W.L. McMillen, a Natchitoches merchant described as being "a quiet, orderly and social gentleman," and George Williams, a prominent citizen, were playing a game of cards when an argument ensued. The argument grew until Williams challenged McMillen to a duel. One cold winter's morning in 1836, the two met behind the American Cemetery. Neither knew the method of dueling and neither was regarded as being good with pistols. They drew and fired at the same time. McMillen's shot missed Williams but Williams hit his target. Williams's ball (shot) entered just above McMillen's right hip and shattered his spine. McMillen lingered for two days before dying from his injuries. McMillen is buried in the American Cemetery just a few feet from where the duel took place.[87]

Many Confederate soldiers were buried in this cemetery but most of their graves were nothing more than "inscriptions mostly written in pencil on wooden head slabs."[88]

- *Across the street at 212 Second Street you will see...*

35. BOOZMAN HOUSE
212 Second Street

This Creole cottage known as the Boozman House was built in about 1900. State Representative Curtis Boozman owned this house. Boozman served two nonconsecutive terms in the Louisiana House of Representatives, first from 1952-1956, and second from 1960-1964.

- *Walk back a block until you read the Judge Porter House and turn right. This will be at the corner of Second Street and Poete Street. Walk along Poete Street until you see on the right...*

36. LAUREATE HOUSE
225 Poete Street

In about 1840, Antonio Balzaretti commissioned Italian architect Anthanese Trizzini and bricklayer Joseph Soldini to build this house.[89] As was common with townhouses, this house was built with outside entrances to each room. In the 1950s, Ruby Smitha Dunckleman, head of economics at Northwestern State University, restored the home.[90] The Laureate House was built with a cellar and a tunnel connecting to Bayou Amulet.[91] (Bayou Amulet connects to Cane River Lake. We will see Bayou Amulet a little later on the tour.)

- *Continue walking along Poete Street until you reach Jefferson Street. Turn right and you will see...*

37. STEEL MAGNOLIAS HOUSE
320 Jefferson Street

In the 1840s, Italian architect Anthanese Trizzini and bricklayer/contractor Joseph Soldini built the Cook-Taylor home for Louis Dupleix, a French immigrant.[92] Until 1908, the building was situated within inches of the street. The sidewalk passed underneath the front porch, with the columns being between the sidewalk and the street. Through the years, this house has been used as a store and Civil War hospital.[93] In 1908, workers transformed this building into the home you see. They disassembled the home, brick-by-brick, and reassembled it 40 feet from the street to increase the size of the front lawn.[94] The original threshold marker with the Taylor family name is embedded in the sidewalk near the location of the original front door. The house features rare round brick columns on the front gallery. The house was fitted with a fallout shelter during the Cold War.[95] It is now called the Steel Magnolias

House.[96] This was the set of the wedding reception and M'Lynn's home in *Steel Magnolias*.[97]

- *Walk to the house to the left of Steel Magnolias House and you will see...*

38. LEMEE HOUSE
310 Jefferson Street

In 1837, Italian architect Anthanese Trizzini and bricklayer/contractor Joseph Soldini built the Lemee house, and included a rare underground brick cellar which was used for preserving foods and wine. Soldini also added a cistern in the cellar which caught and stored rain water for cooking and washing.[98] In 1849, Soldini sold the house to Alexis Lemee, for whom the house is named.[99] Alexis was a representative of and used the Lemee house as a branch of the Union Bank of New Orleans. When the bank went out of business, Alexis used the building as his residence. The house had many owners until 1940, when the City of Natchitoches, recognizing its historic significance, purchased the property.[100] One year later, the Lemee House became the headquarters for the Association for the Preservation of Historic Natchitoches. The Lemee House has a cellar and a tunnel which passes under the street and connects to Cane River Lake.[101]

- *Walk a little further down Jefferson Street and you will see...*

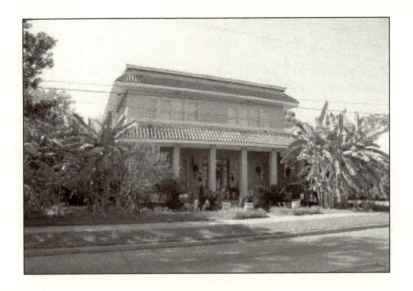

39. SOLDINI HOUSE
240 Jefferson Street

In 1847, bricklayer/contractor Joseph Soldini and Italian architect Anthanese Trizzini built this house as Soldini's town home.[102] Soldini also owned a plantation on Little River about six miles south of Natchitoches.[103] Originally, it was built as a one-and-a-half-story Greek Revival house with galleries along the front and back.[104] In 1858, Soldini sold the home to District Judge Chichester Chaplin and moved to New Orleans. In the 1920s, the Walter Alcock family remodeled the home to accommodate their family of six in the Italian Renaissance style, the way it appears today.[105] This house was built with a full cellar and contains a hidden chamber where the family hid their whiskey still during the Prohibition Era.[106]

- Walk a little further down Jefferson Street and you will see...

40. STEAMBOAT HOUSE
200 Jefferson Street

In the mid-1800s, Judge David Pierson had a stranded and abandoned steamboat lifted from the shallow waters of the Red River (now Cane River Lake) and placed on stone pillars in this location. Judge Pierson modified and added onto the steamboat, and created the aptly-named Steamboat House. For nearly one hundred years, the Steamboat House was divided into apartments and rented to college students. The house has survived several fires. After an upstairs fire on Valentine's Day in 1978, the house was abandoned and remained vacant for several years. In the 1980s, Julia Coleman purchased and restored the Steamboat House. During the renovation process, Ms. Coleman saw the original hull of the boat from underneath the house.[107]

- *Walk a little further down Jefferson Street and you will see...*

41. NELKIN HOUSE
170 Jefferson Street

In 1857, nine-year-old Samuel Nelkin emigrated from Russia. Thirteen years later, fourteen-year-old Sarah Abrams emigrated from Russia.[108] In 1872, Samuel and Sarah married in Natchitoches.[109] Thirty years later, they built this house.[110] Samuel owned and operated a dry goods and grocery store next to this house's current location. He advertised his location as being "below the dirt bridge," which was what we now call the Bayou Amulet bridge.[111]

- *Walk a little further down Jefferson Street and you will see...*

42. DRANGUET HOUSE
146 Jefferson Street

In the 1790s, young Benjamin F. Dranguet fled France with his family during the French Revolution. The Dranguet family settled in Santiago, Cuba. In about 1810, a large number of French political refugees, including the Dranguet family, were expelled by the Cuban government. The Dranguet family then settled in New Orleans. Although he had only been in America a couple of years, Benjamin volunteered and fought in the War of 1812. Following the war, he moved to Natchitoches where he met Mathilde Takusin. Three years later, they married in the Immaculate Conception Church.[112] In about 1835, just two years before his death, Benjamin F. Dranguet built this brick home in the Greek Revival style.[113]

- *Across the street you will see the entrance to…*

43. FORT ST. JEAN BAPTISTE STATE HISTORIC SITE
155 Jefferson Street

Fort St. Jean Baptiste State Historic Site is located a few hundred yards from the location of the original fort. The historic site has a museum and a short video which explains the history of the fort and Natchitoches. Once you have finished inside, take a short walk along the stone path and cross a wooden bridge to step back in time. The recreation of the fort is based on extensive archival research in Louisiana, Canada, and France. Workers used eighteenth century techniques on the approximately 250,000 board feet of lumber to complete the recreation. The palisade wall is made up of nearly 2,000 treated pine logs.

Author's note: I worked as a costumed French Marine at this historic site while earning my bachelor's degree in history from Northwestern State University. I learned many eighteenth century techniques which I shared with visitors including starting a fire using flint and steel, making lead bullets with a bullet mold, demonstrating how to fire flintlock pistols and muskets, making bread in the bread oven, and other daily tasks that soldiers at the fort would have done. For more information on entrance fees and hours, please see the Things To Do in the Historic District section.

- *Cross the street and walk back north along Jefferson Street (Fort St. Jean Baptiste will be on your right) until you see on the left…*

44. WINBARG COTTAGE
210 Jefferson Street

In February, 1923, the home of Natchitoches merchant E.B. Winbarg on Cypress Street was destroyed by fire.[114] Later that same year, Mr. and Mrs. Winbarg built this Mediterranean style stucco home with eleven foot high ceilings and four fireplaces. The home still has its original wood flooring.[115] Alex E. Sompayrac, a farmer and shoe salesman, purchased the house from Winbarg.[116] In 2003, the home was totally renovated with modern conveniences but the original architectural features were preserved.[117]

- *Turn left onto Pine Street. Down on the left you will see...*

45. QUEEN ANNE BED AND BREAKFAST
125 Pine Street

In 1905, Charles J. and Annie Strechan Greene built this Victorian style home. 27 years earlier, Annie immigrated from Scotland, and, four years later, married Charles.[118] In about 1898, they moved to Natchitoches, and raised their five children in this home. Charles was the registrar of the land office at Natchitoches. In 1933, Charles died in this home after a long illness.[119] Annie lived in the home until her death in 1958.[120] Their oldest daughter, Jessie, lived in the house until her death in 1965.[121] After Jessie's death, the house had many owners and was a fraternity house for a while. The house was painstakingly restored and has the original virgin cypress shiplap siding, heart of pine flooring, pocket doors, and bead board ceiling.[122]

- *The next house down is...*

46. GREEN GABLES BED AND BREAKFAST
201 Pine Street

In the 1890s, Estelle Ducournau Plauché had this one-story Queen Anne cottage with center hallway built as a wedding present for her niece.[123] The home features "turned and sawn woodwork on the exterior and a wrap-around porch."[124] The home's ornate fireplaces, stained glass windows, and porch were restored to its original grandeur. The home now operates as a bed and breakfast. Green Gables owner Dr. Ed Kollar, a painter and sculptor, decorated the home with his original artwork.[125]

- *Walk down to the end of Pine Street until you see...*

47. SAMUEL GUY HOUSE
309 Pine Street

In about 1850, Samuel Eldridge Guy built this house on a working plantation near Mansfield, about 50 miles from Natchitoches. [126] On April 8, 1864, the Civil War Battle of Mansfield raged just two miles north of this house.[127] The Guy family nervously peered out of these windows keeping watch for soldiers as the sounds of guns and canons firing filled the air. This two-story Greek Revival home has several unique features to the area including an oversized front entrance and Greek temple dormers. The floor plan is symmetrical with a central hallway with two rooms on each side. The Guy family owned the home for over 150 years. The house sat vacant for many years, had greatly deteriorated, and was in need of total restoration. In 2002, the Joyous Coast Foundation purchased the house in order to preserve it. The house was dismantled, its pieces labeled, and loaded onto five large trucks, and transported to this location for restoration. In 2007, after four laborious years, the restoration of the Samuel Guy House was completed.[128]

- *Walk back along Pine Street (Green Gables and Queen Anne House will be on your right) and turn left onto Jefferson Street. Immediately across the street you will see...*

48. DR. JOHN SIBLEY PARK
Corner of Jefferson Street and Keyser Avenue

Dr. John Sibley was anything but an idle man. During the American Revolution, John Sibley served as a surgeon's mate with the Massachusetts militia. In 1802, Dr. Sibley moved to Natchitoches and provided President Thomas Jefferson with information about the Louisiana territory. In 1805, President Jefferson appointed Dr. Sibley as the Indian agent for the Orleans Territory, which included Natchitoches. He served as Army Post Physician at Fort Claiborne. Dr. Sibley was influential in settling the boundary dispute between the United States and Spain. He served in the Louisiana Senate, as a judge, captain of the militia, and owned and operated multiple local plantations. In 1837, Dr. Sibley died and was buried in the American Cemetery.

- *This is a good **REST STOP**.*
- *Walk back along Jefferson Street two blocks down until you see...*

49. MAISON LOUISIANE
332 Jefferson Street

In the 1852, John Rusca and Maria Theresa Delmonico immigrated to the United States from Switzerland.[129] 23 years later, John and Maria married in Natchitoches.[130] In the 1880s, the Rusca's built Maison Louisiane in the Queen Anne style.[131] John was a merchant and operated his dry goods and grocery store to the left of his home.[132] The house still has its original flooring and thirteen-foot ceilings.[133]

- *Walk north along Jefferson Street until you see…*

50. BAYOU AMULET

Bayou Amulet was originally labelled "Bayou A Mule" on maps because people kept their mules tied up along this spot. Over the years the name evolved into its current name, Bayou Amulet. Natchitoches was originally made up of several islands.[134] Two hundred years ago, Bayou Amulet was a meeting point of French and Spanish traders where goods from New Orleans transported on steamboats met with pack animal trains from Old Mexico.[135] Through changes in transportation, from riverboats to railroad to automobiles, the city added bridges, filled areas in with dirt, and drained the water. Most evidence of the old islands has been removed or is hidden from view with this being the exception. Standing on the Bayou Amulet bridge, you can see the old waterway and where it connected to Cane River Lake.

- *Next to Bayou Amulet is...*

51. LEVY-EAST HOUSE
358 Jefferson Street

Sometime between the 1830s and 1860s, Italian architect Anthanese Trizzini built the original Levy-East House for Dr. Nichola Michel Friedelezy. Dr. Friedelezy practiced medicine from this home until authorities learned that his medical license was a forgery. The disgraced doctor left Natchitoches. Although the house looks like it was built in the 1800s, it is one of the newest houses on the street. In the early morning of June 19, 2012, firefighters responded to fire at the Levy-East House, and found it engulfed in flames.[136] The home was unoccupied at the time of the fire. The house was almost completely destroyed by fire and sustained at least $500,000.00 in damages. Three months later, the State Fire Marshal's Office arrested a woman from Lafayette for intentionally setting the fire that destroyed the Levy-East House.[137] It took nearly five years to rebuild this period-correct home.

- *Next door you will see...*

52. METOYER-BROWN TOWN HOUSE
366 Jefferson Street

In 1850, AntheneseTrizzini and Joseph Soldini built this house for the wealthy Benjamin Metoyer family at a cost of $17,000. Adjusted for inflation, this would be just over a half a million dollars today.[138] Benjamin and Marie Metoyer, along with their twelve children, split their time between their home in the country and this town house. When at their country home, a slave took care of their town house. In 1974, Dr. and Mrs. Steve M. Brown, III, bought and restored the historic home.[139]

- *Walk north along Jefferson Street until you see...*

53. TANTE HUPPÉ HOUSE
424 Jefferson Street

In 1829, Dr. Jean Baptiste Huppé married the twice-widowed, twenty-nine-year-old Suzette Prudhomme Lafon LeCompte.[140] Many in the area affectionately called her "Tante Huppé" (Taunt who-pay), which means Aunt Huppé in French.[141] Shortly after their marriage, Huppé built this two-story, eighteen room house. Shortly after they married, Dr. Huppé died. In her mid-thirties, Tante Huppé was widowed for a third time. Tante Huppé expressed her sadness in a letter to her son, Bernadin, in which she said, "When happiness is all gone, it is a punishment to live."[142] In 1850, shortly after she wrote the letter, her son, Bernadin, died of cholera.[143] Tante Huppé lived alone in the house until her death in 1862.[144]

The walls of the house are made of cypress timbers with bricks laid between them. The exterior was originally covered with a red oxide with white mortar lines painted on top to make the bricks appear larger. The floor is made of 1½ inch thick red pine. Nine fireplaces kept the home warm in winter and eleven outside doors allowed breezes of fresh air to cool it the rest of the year. All of the locks, keys, curtain rods, and glass panes are said to be the originals. The interior is filled with original furnishings and ornate plaster details. The home has some unexplained details such as "two bullet holes in the wall in the front hall and arrowheads in the dining room door." According to local legends, a ghost walks through the house at night while playing a violin.[145] Look on the right brick wall of the house and you will see three iron S's. This is not a decorative feature but an important structural support. A bar or cable is connected to the center of each S and connects to another S on the exact opposite side of the house. These supports keep the bricks from bulging out. Modern bricklayers use hidden clips to secure bricks.

- *Walk north along Jefferson Street until you see...*

54. PRUDHOMME-ROQUIER HOUSE
446 Jefferson Street

In the late 1700s, Jean Baptiste Prudhomme, a royal surgeon educated in France, acquired this parcel of land through a Spanish land grant. In 1778, Francois Rouquier married his daughter, Marie Louise Prudhomme, and received the land from Jean Baptiste Prudhomme as a dowry.[146] Rouquier constructed a bousillage house upon it in the French Creole style.[147] Builders connected cypress beams with wooden pegs to make the floors, walls, rafters, and then filled in the openings with bousillage, a combination of clay and fibrous materials such as deer hair and Spanish moss. Carpenters used cypress doors throughout the home. The Prudhomme-Rouquier house's name stems from the union of Francois Rouquier and Marie Louise Prudhomme. This house is rare because it is the only known example of a two-story bousillage house in the United States.[148] In 1811, Francois died and Marie sold the house to her daughter, Marie Louise Henrietta Rouquier, and son-in-law, Natchitoches Parish Judge John C. Carr.[149]

In 1825, Judge Carr and his wife remodeled the house in the Federal or Greek Revival style.[150] In 1976, the Service League of Natchitoches bought and restored the home to its 1825 style. The Service League offers tours by appointment only and leases the building and courtyard for weddings and weddings receptions. Call 318-352-6723 for more information.

- *Walk north along Jefferson Street until you get to Front Street and you will see...*

55. DON THEATER
507 Front Street

In 1916, the newly formed Natchitoches Opera Company began construction on a steel and brick building to house their productions.[151] A previous Natchitoches Opera House was torn down in 1891.[152] Within a few years, the opera house evolved into the Amusu Theater. In February, 1924, a large number of the citizenry went to the Amusu Theater for a memorial service in honor of the recently deceased President Woodrow Wilson.[153] In the 1950s, it became the Don Theater. At the time, movie theaters, including this one, were segregated. "Colored" people purchased tickets at the front of the building, and then had to enter the theater through a side door, climb the stairs to balcony, and find their assigned seats. They were not allowed to use the inside concession stand and had to purchase refreshments outside.[154] The Don Theater closed in the 1980s when a larger, multiple-screen theater opened in another part of town. The theater has been repurposed as condominiums.

- *Next to the Don Theater you will see...*

56. OLD NAKATOSH HOTEL
Corner of Front Street and Church Street

In about 1906, the Alphonse Prudhomme and Elisa Lecomte families built what was originally a two story hotel at this prime location. A third story was later added. It was originally called the Lecomte Hotel. In 1920, W.P. Wemp purchased the hotel and renamed it the Wemp Hotel. Five years later, L.H. Johnson purchased the hotel and renamed it the Old Nakatosh Hotel.[155] Today, the Old Nakatosh Hotel has retail spaces on the first floor and condominiums on the upper floors.

- *Turn right and cross over Cane River Lak on the Church Street Bridge. Turn left onto Williams Avenue.*
- *A note of caution: The next two stops on the tour do not have consistent sidewalk access.*

57. TAUZIN-WELLS HOUSE
607 Williams Avenue

Patrick Murphy built this home for his daughter and son-in-law, Joseph Tauzin, during the American Revolution.[156] This explains the first part of this home's current name. The home is believed to be the oldest surviving building in Natchitoches and the second oldest residence west of the Mississippi River.[157] Like several other homes in the Historic District, this Creole Cottage was built with cypress sills and rafters, held together by wooden pegs, and filled in with bousillage.[158] The logs used in the construction of the home were cut and floated downstream to Natchitoches. Slaves sawed the cypress lumber by hand in the river, as was common before sawmills existed in the area. "It took four years to float the logs, saw the lumber, and build the house." The home originally contained a store which was a trading post between Natchez, Mississippi, and Mexico. "Deer and fur bearing animals were brought to this store and sold and tanned on the premises." It originally had a gallery which wrapped around the perimeter of the house. The rear and side galleries were eventually enclosed to increase the living space.[159] In 1969, Dr. Thomas Wells, history professor of Northwestern State University, restored the home to its original condition.[160] This explains the second part of this home's current name.

- *Continue walking along Williams Avenue until you see on your right...*

58. ROSELAWN
905 Williams Avenue

The first thing you notice when you approach Roselawn is the long two-tone green fence that stretches along the front and side of the property. The beautiful Roselawn house is mostly hidden from view by large Magnolia trees. The image above shows Roselawn as you will be able to see it from outside the fence. This is a private residence. In 1894, J. Henry Williams and his brother-in-law, R.E. Milling bought a fifty acre tract of land which was once leased by the Natchitoches Jockey Club, a horseracing club.[161] The Lecomte Race Track was located on this site.[162] The following year, Henry bought his brother-in-law's half of the property. It was here in 1903 when 48-year-old Henry built the home for his 32-year-old bride, Marie Eliza Conrnelia Payne.[163] The Williams family purchased the blueprints and supplies list from one of many catalogues published by architect George Barber. The supplies were delivered to Natchitoches on the Texas and Pacific Railway.[164] The home is one of the best examples of Queen Anne Revival style in the entire state. Although the home is called Roselawn, it is sometimes referred to as the Painted Lady because of its nine different paint colors ranging from shades of green to tan, the same colors it was painted when new. Roselawn has a 134-foot wraparound gallery that covers the front and sides of the home. The home is still owned by the Williams family.[165]

- *Take a look down Williams Avenue at the Oak trees that line the road. This is a favorite spot for pictures.*

- *This concludes the Historic District Walking Tour. To return to Front Street, walk back in the direction of the Tauzin-Wells House and turn right at the bridge.*

THINGS TO DO IN THE HISTORIC DISTRICT

Cane River Brewing Company

Cane River Paddle & Pedal Sports
If you are interested in a high energy experience, you can rent a paddle board, kayak, stand up peddle board, or hydro bike, and explore Cane River Lake.
Address: Beau Fort Station located next to the stage on the Riverbank.
Hours: Tuesday - Wednesday: Call for an appointment. Thursday - Saturday: 12 pm – 7 pm, Sunday: 1 pm – 7 pm. (318) 527-0066

Cane River Paddle Queen

Carriage Rides by Natchitoches Tour Company
Take a nice, relaxing ride in a horse-drawn carriage through the Historic District. For the first two hundred years of its existence, people in Natchitoches travelled in carriages much like these. The driver gives a guided tour and details historic sites and *Steel Magnolias* filming sites.
Hours: Hours vary seasonally and depend on the weather. Usually March-August from about 10 am until 2 pm, September and October from about 10 am until 4 pm. November and December are usually from around 4pm until 9 pm.
Address: Look for the carriages parked on Front Street in the Historic District. No tickets are necessary. Just pay the driver. (318) 214-7733.

Fort St. Jean Baptiste State Historic Site
Step back into the 1700s French Colonial Louisiana in this reproduction of Fort St. Jean Baptiste. A short film explains the relationship between the French and Indians in and around Natchitoches. The museum has a wonderful interactive diorama which depicts how the Fort and land surrounding the Fort looked in the 1700s. Twice a year, in March and December, the Fort hosts encampments featuring period costumed re-enactors, sutlers selling merchandise in temporary tents, canon firing demonstrations and musket firing demonstrations. Call for exact dates.
Hours: Wednesday-Sunday, 9 am to 5 pm. Closed on Thanksgiving, Christmas and New Year's Day.
Address: 155 Jefferson Street. (318) 357-3101 or 1-888-677-7853.

Kaffie-Frederick General Mercantile Store
Kaffie-Frederick's, as locals call it, is like a museum and functioning store all rolled up into one. Along with fine merchandise, look for vintage photographs throughout the store.
Hours: Monday-Saturday, 8 am to 5 pm. Closed Sunday.
Address: 758 Front Street. Tel. 318-352-2525.
www.oldhardwarestore.com.

Live Music in the Historic District
Natchitoches is home to some fine, talented musicians. Several of the restaurants in the Historic District host live music on Thursday, Friday, and Saturday nights. The Historic District holds many festivals throughout the year, all of which have local live musicians playing for your enjoyment.

Louisiana Sports Hall of Fame and Northwest Louisiana History Museum

This museum has something for everyone. Sports exhibits include memorabilia, high-definition videos, life stories told on touch screen displays, and much more. The History Museum contains artifacts all the way back to the 1700s showing aspects of the lives of the French, Spanish, Indians, and Americans in the area. The museum highlights twelve paintings by internationally renowned folk artist Clementine Hunter.

Hours: Open 10 am to 4:30 pm, Tuesday-Saturday. Closed Sundays, Mondays, and state holidays.
Address: 800 Front Street, Natchitoches.
Tel. 318-357-2492. www.lasportshall.com.

Nakatosh Tattoo Gallery

Get a new tattoo at the only tattoo gallery in the Historic District. Their facilities are clean and their work is superb. You must be at least 18 years old. Regardless of your age, **bring your ID.**

Hours: Tuesday – Thursday, 12 pm – 9 pm, Friday and Saturday, 12 pm - 10 pm, Sunday, 2 pm – 8 pm. Closed Mondays.
Address: 119 St. Denis Street. Tel. 318-238-6824.

FESTIVALS IN THE HISTORIC DISTRICT

Bloomin' on the Bricks/Art Along the Bricks
March, 2020
This is two festivals in one. **Bloomin' on the Bricks** is a celebration of spring and garden festival. The Historic District will be in bloom with hanging flower baskets and thousands of tulips and daffodils on display. There will be a host of lawn and garden vendors, live musical entertainment, and children's activities. **Art Along the Bricks** is a celebration of local arts and crafts. Local artists display their creations in an outdoor art show. **Admission to this event is free.** For more information visit www.DownTownNatchitoches.com.

Natchitoches Christmas Festival
Mid-November – First Weekend in January
The Christmas Festival is Natchitoches's most popular event with over 300,000 Christmas lights and over 100 Riverbank set pieces. To facilitate the large number of visitors to the Historic District, the Christmas lights are turned on at dusk every night from mid-November the first weekend in January. On the first Saturday in December, locals and tourists alike will be in town for the Annual Christmas Festival. The Festival of Lights Parade begins at 1 pm. Entertainers perform on the Riverbank throughout the day. The Fireworks Over Cane River Lake begins at 6 pm. Entertainers continue performing after the fireworks. Bring lawn chairs, blankets, and plenty of Christmas spirit. **Armbands must be purchased to enter Front Street and the Riverbank**. For more information visit www.natchitocheschristmas.com.

Natchitoches Classic Car Show
Fall, 2020
Hundreds of vehicles are put on display at the Natchitoches Classic Car Show each year. This is one of the largest classic car shows in the state. Antique and classic vehicles park along Front Street and the Riverbank. You may be able to point out a car you once owned. Local bands perform along several stages intermingled with the cars. All of the shops will be open for this busy shopping day in the Historic District. Bring lawn chairs, a camera, and maybe even your own classic car. If you have been dreaming of buying a classic car, you can drive one home. Some of the cars will be for sale. Admission to this event is free. For more information visit www.natchitochescarshow.com.

Natchitoches Jazz and R&B Festival
Spring, 2020
This huge festival held on the Riverbank showcases several genres of music on multiple stages including, Jazz, Rhythm and Blues, Country, Zydeco, Blues, and rock and roll. In addition to a host of local performers, past performers include Edgar Winter, the Marshall Tucker Band, Eddie Money, the Atlanta Rhythm Section, .38 Special, Mitch Ryder, and Trombone Shorty.
Get ready to clap your hands, dance, and sing along. Bring lawn chairs and a blanket. For a list of artists and to purchase armbands visit www.natchjazzfest.com.

EATING AND DRINKING IN THE HISTORIC DISTRICT

The Cakery
Bakery, cupcakes, custom cakes.
108 Touline Street
318-238-3939

Cane Rio Cafe
Wide variety of Mexican and American foods.
105 Church Street
318-238-3555

Cane River Brewing Company
Spacious taproom and brewery in a former cotton gin building from the 1920s. Cane River Brewing Company frequently hosts live bands. Tour the brewery on Saturdays. Call for more information.
108 Mill Street
318-238-2739

Cane River Candy Company
Wide variety of candies, taffy, gummy bears, pecans, etc.
760 Front Street
318-238-3024

Front Street Market Place
Wide variety of coffees and snacks.
584 Front Street
318-238-3030

Hana Japanese Sushi Bar & Grill

Asian cuisine.
750 Front Street
318-356-0989

The Landing Restaurant & Bar
American, Seafood, Gluten free options.
The Landing usually has live music on the weekends.
530 Front Street
318-352-1579

Lasyone's Meat Pie Kitchen
Creole and Cajun food.
622 Second Street
318-352-3353

The Loft at Five Thirty
Beer, Darts, Pool, Music
530 Front Street
318-652-6694

Maglieux's Riverfront Restaurant
Italian, American, Seafood, Vegetarian Friendly, Gluten Free Options. Maglieux's usually has live music on the weekends.
805 Washington Street
318-354-7767

Mama's Oyster House and Blues Room
Seafood, American food. Mama's usually has live music on the weekends.
608 Front Street
318-356-7874

Mayeaux's Steak & Seafood
Steakhouse, Seafood, Wine bar.
512 Front Street
318-521-8080

Merci Beaucoup
Cajun and Creole, Gluten Free Options, Vegetarian Friendly.
127 Church Street
318-352-6634

Papa's Bar & Grill
American food.
604 Front Street
318-356-7874

Pioneer Pub
American, Seafood, pub food. Pioneer Pub usually has live music on the weekends.
812 Washington Street
318-352-4884

Sweet Fruit Delights
Edible arrangements, caramel apples, chocolate covered strawberries, and other sweets which are almost too beautiful to eat…almost.
628 Front Street
318-352-5910

SHOPPING IN THE HISTORIC DISTRICT

ANTIQUES

Cora's Antiques & Gifts
754 Front Street
318-354-7900

Front Street Antiques & Collectibles
512 Front Street
318-228-8215

Tres Bien Antiques
132 St. Denis Street
(318) 228-8815

ART GALLERIES

Cane River Gallery & Custom Frame Shop
558 Front Street
318-352-0034

Natchitoches Art Guild Heritage Gallery
584 Front Street, Suite 102
318-352-1626

CLOTHING

Brenda's Clothing & Accessories
103 Church Street
318-356-0422

Hall Tree
600 Front Street
318-352-4177

Hello Dolly
520 Front Street
318-352-5828

Razzle Dazzle Boutique
584 Front Street
318-354-9887

Simply Chic Boutique
502 Front Street
318-521-8009

FLORISTS

Jeanne's Country Garden (Florist)
300 Jefferson Street
318-357-0102

Mary Lou's Flowers & Gifts
117 St. Denis Street
318-357-1160

NATCHITOCHES HISTORIC DISTRICT WALKING TOUR

GIFTS & HOME ACCESSORIES

Bathhouse Soapery & Caldarium
506 Front Street
(318) 238-7627

Cane River Kitchenware
732 Front Street
(318) 238-3600

Clary's Christmas Company
548 Front Street
318-238-4582

Dickens & Co.
524 Front Street
318-352-1993

Immaculate Conception Catholic Church Gift Shop
613 Second Street
318-352-1156

Georgia's Gift Shop
626 Front Street
318-352-5833

Gift's Galore & More
113 St. Denis Street
318-352-3831

Kaffie-Frederick General Mercantile
758 Front Street
318-352-2525

Louisiana Purchase
550 Front Street
318-352-0117

Merci Beaucoup Gift Shop
107 Church Street
318-352-6624

Olivier's Fine Louisiana-Style Cypress Furniture
115 Second Street
Also located in the carriageway between 754 and 732 Front Street.
318-352-1427

Plantation Treasures
720 Front Street
318-354-1714

Southern Necessities
624 Front Street
318-354-8808

Vintage Magnolia
780 Front Street
318-238-3870

GUIDED TOURS

Tours by Jan (Frederick)
Historic District, Steel Magnolias Locations Tours, Cane River Plantation tours
(318) 352-2324 or (318) 471-9505

Tour Natchitoches with Barbara (Bailey)
Downtown Historic Tour, Steel Magnolias Tour, Melrose and/or Oakland Plantation Tour
(318) 663-5468 or (318) 663-5469
www.tournatchitocheswithbarbara.com

HAIR CARE

All Tangled Up: A Full Service Family Salon
516 Front Street
Appointments recommended. 318-356-7955

City Barber Shop
504 Front Street
318-352-9500

Cut It Up
141 St. Denis Street
(318) 356-8881

Scarlett's Southern Beauties Salon
Lafayette Street (Across from Louisiana Sports Hall of Fame)
(318) 228-8239

INFORMATION

Natchitoches Area Chamber of Commerce
373 Second Street
318-352-6894

Visitor Information Center
780 Front Street, Suite 100
1-800-259-1714

MISCELLANEOUS

Cane River Paddle & Pedal Sports
780 Front Street, Suite 104
(318) 527-0066

Cane River Queen Riverboat
103 Rue Beauport
318-663-7787

Nakatosh Tattoo Co.
119 St. Denis Street
(318) 238-OUCH

SPAS

La Petite Maison Day Spa
131 Amulet Street
Phone: (318) 354-0505

Magnolia Spa & Wellness
131 Touline Street
(318) 238-2843

Wall Rejuvenation Center & Medical Spa
780 Front Street, Suite 106
(318) 352-2250

SLEEPING IN THE HISTORIC DISTRICT

When visiting the Natchitoches Historic District, you can stay in a bed and breakfast, guest house, townhouse, log cabin, or a hotel. There are many to choose from. For best results, book your choice of the following as soon as possible. Natchitoches is always busy with tourists, and rooms get booked up quickly. Keep in mind that room rates increase during special events and holidays. Prices in this book were taken directly from the listing's website or directly from the owner.

1. Andre's Riverview Bed and Breakfast
1950s three-story cottage overlooking Cane River Lake.
612 Williams Avenue
For booking, call 318-581-0287 or visit www.andresriverview.com.

2. Andrew Morris House Bed and Breakfast
An antebellum planter's cottage built around 1855.
422 Second Street
For booking, call 1-800-441-8343 or visit www.andrewmorrishouse.com.

3. Cabin on Cane River
A log cabin guest house built in 1935 on the banks of the Cane River Lake.
614 Williams Avenue
For booking, call 318-527-9709 or visit www.cabinoncaneriver.com.

4. Chateau Saint Denis Hotel
The newest place to stay in the Historic District.
751 Second Street
For booking, call 1-888-900-9937 or visit www.chateausaintdenis.com.

5. Church Street Inn
20 uniquely decorated rooms, guests-only patio and balcony.
120 Church Street
For booking, call 1-800-668-9298 or visit www.churchstinn.com.

6. The Cottage Guest House
French Creole cottage built in the 1850s.
824 Second Street
For booking, call (318) 352-8744.

7. Creole Cottage Bed and Breakfast
200 year old cottage overlooking Cane River Lake.
319 Jefferson Street
For booking, call 318-413-0579, email ccpage@bellsouth.net, or visit www.creolecottage.net.

8. Ducournau Townhouse
Second floor townhouse built in 1835 with balcony overlooking Front Street.
752 Front Street
For booking, call 318-352-1774.

9. Good House Bed and Breakfast
English cottage built in 1930.
314 Poete Street
For booking, call 318-332-5195 or visit www.rutledgepropertiesbandb.com.

10. Green Gables Bed and Breakfast and Camellia Cottage
One-story Victorian cottage built in the 1890s.
201 Pine Street
For booking, call 318-352-5580 or visit www.virtualcities.com/la/greengables.htm.

11. H.A. Cook Guesthouse
Guest house with French doors leading to a private balcony.
128 St. Denis Street
For booking, call 225-802-8704 or visit www.vrbo.com/675761.

12. Jefferson House Bed and Breakfast
Pet friendly house overlooking Cane River Lake.
229 Jefferson Street
For booking, call 1-866-254-7279 or visit www.jeffersonhousebedandbreakfast.com.

13. Jefferson Street Townhouse
Finely decorated with antiques, and has a swimming pool.
230 Jefferson Street
For booking, call 1-800-342-3957 or visit www.jeffersontownhouse.com.

14. Judge Porter House Bed and Breakfast
Queen Anne influenced architecture, wraparound two-story gallery.
321 Second Street
For booking, call 1-800-441-8343 or visit www.judgeporterhouse.com.

15. La Maison Louisiane Bed and Breakfast
Victorian home finely decorated with antiques.
322 Jefferson Street
For booking, call 318-332-8780.

16. Parsonage Bed and Breakfast
Former Methodist parsonage built in the 1940s.
307 Percy Street
For booking, call 318-214-9607 or visit www.parsonagebedandbreakfast.com.

17. Queen Anne Bed and Breakfast
Victorian home built in 1905.
125 Pine Street
For booking, call 1-800-441-8343 or visit www.queenannebandb.com.

18. Rusca House Bed and Breakfast
1920s bungalow with formal gardens
124 Poete Street
For booking, call 1-866-531-0898 or visit www.ruscahouse.com.

19. Samuel Guy House Bed and Breakfast
Two-story 1850s plantation home with large ornate entrance and porch.
309 Pine Street
For booking, call 1-800-984-1080 or visit www.samuelguyhouse.com.

20. Steel Magnolias House Bed and Breakfast
1830s home used in the filming of *Steel Magnolias*.
320 Jefferson Street
For booking, call 318-332-8780.

21. Sweet Cane Inn Bed and Breakfast
Built for a Congressman in the late 1800s. Supposedly haunted.
926 Washington Street
Children over the age of 15 are allowed.
For booking, call 225-226-8820 or visit www.sweetcaneinn.com.

22. Vera's Guest House
Servants' house built in the 1860s with private dock overlooking Cane River Lake.
907 Washington Street
For booking, call 318-609-0110 or visit www.verashouse.com.

23. Violet Hill Bed and Breakfast
Victorian home built in the late 1800s overlooking Cane River Lake.
917 Washington Street
For booking, call 1-866-357-0858 or visit www.violethillbandb.com.

ABOUT THE AUTHOR

Brad Dison was born, raised, and lives near the small village of Saline, Louisiana. He earned a bachelor's degree in history from Northwestern State University in Natchitoches, Louisiana, and a master's degree in history from Louisiana Tech University in Ruston, Louisiana. His other works include articles published in scholarly journals on topics of North Louisiana history, and books entitled *Bienville Parish: Images of America,* and *Whiskey and Blood, The Story of Four Louisiana Law Enforcement Officers Killed by Bootleggers During Prohibition.*

NOTES

[1] The Shreveport *Times*, February 26, 1928, p. 8.
[2] The New Orleans *Times-Democrat*, May 10, 1886, p. 8.
[3] The Shreveport *Times*, February 26, 1928, p. 8.
[4] New Orleans *Louisiana State Gazette*, March 27, 1820, p. 2.
[5] The New Orleans *Times-Picayune*, March 15, 1843, p. 2.
[6] The Shreveport *Times*, September 8, 1916, p. 3.
[7] The Shreveport *Times*, March 3, 1917, p. 2.
[8] The Shreveport *Times*, October 19, 1917, p. 4.
[9] The Shreveport *Times*, November 11, 1917, p. 8.
[10] The Shreveport *Times*, May 25, 1998, p. 19.
[11] The Shreveport *Times*, October 24, 1958, p. 34.
[12] The Shreveport *Times*, November 13, 2008, p. 4.
[13] "Buried History Found under Natchitoches' Front Street Bricks," June 12, 2008, https://www.ktbs.com/news/buried-history-found-under-natchitoches-front-street-bricks/article_1ce49635-59d9-53ec-b109-0dd229d253d3.html, accessed August 31, 2017.
[14] The Shreveport *Times*, November 13, 2008, p. 4.
[15] The Alexandria *Town Talk*, March 21, 1971, p. 7.
[16] The Alexandria *Town Talk*, April 28, 1967, p. 4.
[17] The Alexandria *Town Talk*, September 6, 1973, p. 23.
[18] The Alexandria *Town Talk*, September 24, 1967, p. 14.
[19] Joyous Coast Foundation, *Images of America: Natchitoches* (Charleston: Arcadia Publishing, 2003), 37.
[20] The Abbeville *Meridional*, March 7, 1891, p. 2.
[21] The Opelousas *Courier*, April 18, 1891, p. 1.
[22] http://www.violethillbandb.com/history1.htm.
[23] Martin, Maggie, "Steel Magnolias still impacts town after 25 years," the Shreveport *Times*, October 2, 2014, http://www.shreveporttimes.com/story/news/local/louisiana/2014/10/02/steel-magnolias-still-impacts-town-years/16604503/, accessed September 4, 2017.
[24] Shreveport *Times*, April 30, 1934, p. 1.
[25] Martin, Maggie, "Are There Ghosts in Natchitoches," the Shreveport *Times*, April 24, 2016, http://www.shreveporttimes.com/story/life/community/2016/04/24/there-ghosts-natchitoches/82794174/, accessed September 4, 2017.

[26] Julia Coleman, interviewed by author, Natchitoches, LA, November 8, 2017.
[27] Shreveport *Times*, October 14, 1962, p. 64.
[28] "Menu," Pioneer Pub, accessed September 21, 2017, https://www.zomato.com/natchitoches-la/pioneer-pub-natchitoches/menu.
[29] Monroe *News-Star*, June 26, 2016, p. A17.
[30] Natchitoches Populist, April 30, 1897, p. 3.
[31] Monroe *News-Star*, December 26, 2015, p. B2.
[32] Lafayette *Gazette*, August 20, 1898, p. 1.
[33] Natchitoches *People's Vindicator*, December 25, 1875, p. 3.
[34] Natchitoches *People's Vindicator*, December 26, 1874, p. 2.
[35] Natchitoches *People's Vindicator*, September 1, 1877, p. 1.
[36] Shreveport *Times*, October 7, 1978, p. 10.
[37] Shreveport *Times*, May 16, 1976, p. 29.
[38] http://www.laspirits.com/PDFs/Businesses/PlantationTreasures.pdf
[39] New Orleans *Times Picayune*, January 8, 1876, p. 5.
[40] New Orleans *Times Democrat*, December 29, 1875, p. 1.
[41] New Orleans *Republican*, January 8, 1876, p. 5.
[42] Shreveport *Times*, November 12, 1922, p. 1.
[43] Shreveport *Times*, November 12, 1922, p. 1.
[44] Alexandria *Town Talk*, November 16, 1922, p. 1.
[45] Alexandria *Town Talk*, December 20, 1922, p. 1.
[46] Alexandria *Town Talk*, September 29, 1923, p. 5.
[47] Alexandria *Weekly Town Talk*, November 10, 1934, p. 11.
[48] Alexandria *Town Talk*, October 4, 1992, p. 33.
[49] Alexandria *Town Talk*, July 16, 1972, p. 19.
[50] Alexandria *Weekly Town Talk*, November 10, 1934, p. 11.
[51] Joyous Coast Foundation, *Images of America: Natchitoches* (Charleston: Arcadia Publishing, 2003, 70.
[52] "Immaculate Conception Catholic Church," Natchitoches.net, accessed October 13, 2017, http://www.natchitoches.net/attractions/historic-district/immaculate-conception-catholic-church/.
[53] "Bishop Augustus Marie Martin," Catholic Hierarchy, accessed October 13, 2017, http://www.catholic-hierarchy.org/bishop/bmartina.html.

54 Shreveport *Times*, June 8, 1996, p. 18.
55 Petrus, Jeannie, "The Church Today," vol. XXXIX, No. 4, April 20, 2009, http://www.holymotherchurch.org/files/37466174.pdf, accessed September 10, 2017.
56 Alexandria *Town Talk*, April 29, 1940, p. 3.
57 Shreveport *Times*, May 3, 1953, p. 20.
58 Alexandria *Town Talk*, January 30, 1972, p. 24.
59 Alexandria *Weekly Town Talk*, December 15, 1934, p. 7.
60 Alexandria *Town Talk*, April 8, 1987, p. 24.
61 Alexandria *Town Talk*, July 4, 2015, p. A3.
62 New Orleans *Times-Democrat*, April 26, 1904, p. 11.
63 New Orleans *Times-Democrat*, September 16, 1904, p. 8.
64 Donaldsonville *Chief*, September 24, 1904, p. 1.
65 Shreveport *Times*, May 24, 1994, p. 7.
66 Alexandria *Town Talk*, September 18, 1994, p. 31.
67 El Dorado *News-Times*, November 2, 1974, p. 9.
68 El Dorado *News-Times*, November 2, 1974, p. 9.
69 http://trinityparish.info/about-us/history/, accessed September 11, 2017.
70 Shreveport *Times*, October 9, 1983, p. 4.
71 Joyous Coast Foundation, *Images of America: Natchitoches* (Charleston: Arcadia Publishing, 2003), 38.
72 "Urbanization," Texas State Historical Association, accessed October 7, 2017, https://tshaonline.org/sites/default/files/images/handbook/TT/texas-pacific-railroad.jpg.
73 Shreveport *Times*, June 21, 1927, p. 16.
74 http://www.masonsalters.com/history, Accessed September 15, 2017.
75 http://www.judgeporterhouse.com/specials.htm, accessed September 15, 2017.
76 United States Federal Census 1880, 1900, 1920.
77 New Orleans *Times-Democrat*, June 10, 1906, p. 6.
78 Alexandria, *Weekly Town Talk*, September 2, 1922, p. 4.
79 Ruston *Daily Leader*, March 3, 1934, p. 1.
80 Alexandria *Town Talk*, April 29, 1940, p. 3.
81 New Orleans *Times Picayune*, September 10, 1884, p. 8.
82 New Orleans *Times Picayune*, April 26, 1889, p. 4.

[83] Shreveport *Times*, May 7, 1939, p. 1.
[84] Alexandria *Town Talk*, April 29, 1940, p. 3.
[85] New Orleans *Times Picayune*, April 26, 1889, p. 4.
[86] Ruston *Daily Leader*, March 3, 1934, p. 1.
[87] Natchitoches *People's Vindicator*, December 21, 1878, p. 3.
[88] New Orleans *Times Picayune*, April 26, 1889, p. 4.
[89] El Dorado *News-Times*, November 2, 1974, p. 9.
[90] Joyous Coast Foundation, *Images of America: Natchitoches* (Charleston: Arcadia Publishing, 2003), 40.
[91] 63rd Annual Fall Pilgrimage Natchitoches Underground (Natchitoches: Association for the Preservation of Historic Natchitoches, 2017).
[92] Alexandria *Town Talk*, December 6, 1981, p. 55.
[93] Alexandria *Town Talk*, December 6, 1981, p. 55.
[94] Gresham, Tom, Jerry Pierce and Tom Whitehead, Steel Magnolias Scrapbook, NSU Press, Natchitoches, LA, 1989, p. 21.
[95] 63rd Annual Fall Pilgrimage Natchitoches Underground (Natchitoches: Association for the Preservation of Historic Natchitoches, 2017).
[96] Alexandria *Town Talk*, December 6, 1981, p. 55.
[97] Shreveport *Times*, October 3, 2014, p. E10.
[98] Shreveport *Times*, February 4, 1977, p. 22.
[99] Alexandria *Town Talk*, October 9, 1956, p. 15.
[100] Shreveport *Times*, February 4, 1977, p. 22.
[101] 63rd Annual Fall Pilgrimage Natchitoches Underground (Natchitoches: Association for the Preservation of Historic Natchitoches, 2017).
[102] Shreveport *Times*, October 5, 2016, p. D4.
[103] Semi-Weekly Natchitoches Times, December 5, 1866, p. 3.
[104] Joyous Coast Foundation, *Images of America: Natchitoches* (Charleston: Arcadia Publishing, 2003), 27.
[105] Shreveport *Times*, August 2, 2004, p. 13.
[106] 63rd Annual Fall Pilgrimage Natchitoches Underground (Natchitoches: Association for the Preservation of Historic Natchitoches, 2017).
[107] Julia Coleman, interviewed by author, Natchitoches, LA, November 8, 2017.

[108] "1920 United States Federal Census," Ancestry.com, accessed September 19, 2017, https://www.ancestry.com/interactive/7602/4120184_00563?pid=5962276&backurl=http://search.ancestry.com/cgi-bin/sse.dll?_phsrc%3DVXC32%26_phstart%3DsuccessSource%26usePUBJs%3Dtrue%26gss%3Dangs-g%26new%3D1%26rank%3D1%26gsfn%3Dsarah%.

[109] "1920 United States Federal Census," Ancestry.com, accessed September 19, 2017, https://www.ancestry.com/interactive/7602/4120184_00563?pid=5962276&backurl=http://search.ancestry.com/cgi-bin/sse.dll?_phsrc%3DVXC32%26_phstart%3DsuccessSource%26usePUBJs%3Dtrue%26gss%3Dangs-g%26new%3D1%26rank%3D1%26gsfn%3Dsarah%.

[110] Joyous Coast Foundation, *Images of America: Natchitoches* (Charleston: Arcadia Publishing, 2003), 29.

[111] Natchitoches *People's Vindicator*, July 14, 1877, p. 1.

[112] "Benjamin Felix Dranguet," Find A Grave, accessed September 19, 2017, https://findagrave.com/cgi-bin/fg.cgi?page=gr&GSln=dranguet&GSbyrel=all&GSdyrel=all&GSst=20&GScnty=1143&GScntry=4&GSob=n&GRid=93296213&df=all&.

[113] Joyous Coast Foundation, *Images of America: Natchitoches* (Charleston: Arcadia Publishing, 2003), 30.

[114] Shreveport *Times*, February 24, 1923, p. 11.

[115] "Winbarg Cottage," InnShopper.com, accessed October 7, 2017, https://www.innshopper.com/ViewListing.aspx?ListingID=1112.

[116] Alexandria *Town Talk*, February 9, 1966, p. 5.

[117] "Winbarg Cottage," InnShopper.com, accessed October 7, 2017, https://www.innshopper.com/ViewListing.aspx?ListingID=1112.

[118] "1900 United States Federal Census for Chas. J. Greene," Ancestry.com, accessed September 19, 2017, https://www.ancestry.com/interactive/7602/4120184_00560?pid=5962110&backurl=http://search.ancestry.com/cgi-bin/sse.dll?_phsrc%3DVXC39%26_phstart%3DsuccessSource%26usePUBJs%3Dtrue%26gss%3Dangs-g%26new%3D1%26rank%3D1%26msT%3D1%26gsf.

[119] Alexandria *Town Talk*, April 14, 1933, p. 10.
[120] Shreveport *Times*, July 25, 1958, p. 28.
[121] Shreveport *Times*, November 28, 1965, p. 31.
[122] http://www.queenannebandb.com/History.htm, accessed September 16, 2017.
[123] http://virtualcities.com/la/greengables.htm, accessed September 16, 2017.
[124] Shreveport *Times*, November 24, 2001, p. 32.
[125] http://virtualcities.com/la/greengables.htm, accessed September 16, 2017.
[126] http://www.samuelguyhouse.com/, accessed September 16, 2017.
[127] Joyous Coast Foundation, *Images of America: Natchitoches* (Charleston: Arcadia Publishing, 2003), 4.
[128] http://www.samuelguyhouse.com/, accessed September 16, 2017.
[129] "1910 U.S. Federal Census for John A. Rusca," Ancestry.com, accessed September 19, 2017, https://www.ancestry.com/interactive/7884/31111_4329980-01094?pid=9239950&backurl=http://search.ancestry.com/cgi-bin/sse.dll?_phsrc%3DVXC18%26_phstart%3DsuccessSource%26usePUBJs%3Dtrue%26gss%3Dangs-g%26new%3D1%26rank%3D1%26msT%3D1.
[130] "Louisiana Marriages, 1718-1925," Ancestry.com, accessed September 19, 2017, http://search.ancestry.com/cgi-bin/sse.dll?_phsrc=VXC18&_phstart=successSource&usePUBJs=true&gss=angs-g&new=1&rank=1&msT=1&gsfn=giovanni&gsfn_x=0&gsln=rusca&gsln_x=1&msypn__ftp=natchitoches&cp=0&catbucket=rstp&MSAV=1&uidh=i5d&pcat.
[131] Joyous Coast Foundation, *Images of America: Natchitoches* (Charleston: Arcadia Publishing, 2003), 25.
[132] Joyous Coast Foundation, *Images of America: Natchitoches* (Charleston: Arcadia Publishing, 2003), 25.
[133] Shreveport *Times*, November 24, 2001, p. 32.
[134] Carte de l Etablissement Francois Sur La Riviere Rouge, https://greatriver.smugmug.com/Art/New-Handpainted-Historic-Maps/i-XkpBpcH/L, accessed September 16, 2017.
[135] Shreveport *Times*, October 26, 1928, p. 28.

[136] Lafayette *Daily Advertiser*, June 20, 2012, p. 14.
[137] Shreveport *Times*, September 25, 2012, p. 3.
[138] "1850 dollars in 2017," Inflation Calculator, accessed September 18, 2017, http://www.in2013dollars.com/1850-dollars-in-2017?amount=17000.
[139] "Metoyer-Brown Town," Natchitohes.net, accessed September 18, 2017, http://www.natchitoches.net/attractions/historic-district/metoyer-brown-town-house/.
[140] "Louisiana, Compiled Marriages, 1728-1850," Ancestry.com, accessed September 18, 2017, http://search.ancestry.com/cgi-bin/sse.dll?_phsrc=VXC14&_phstart=successSource&usePUBJs=true&gss=angs-g&new=1&rank=1&msT=1&gsfn=suzette&gsfn_x=0&gsln=huppe&gsln_x=1&msypn__ftp=natchitoches&msbdy=1799&cp=0&catbucket=rstp&MSAV=1&uid.
[141] Shreveport *Times*, October 11, 1970, p. 66.
[142] Shreveport *Times*, October 11, 1970, p. 74.
[143] Shreveport *Times*, October 11, 1970, p. 66.
[144] Jackson *Clarion-Ledger*, January 7, 1979, p. 59.
[145] Jackson *Clarion-Ledger*, January 7, 1979, p. 59.
[146] "Prudhomme-Roquier House," Cane River National Heritage Area, accessed September 17, 2017, https://www.nps.gov/nr/travel/caneriver/pru.htm.
[147] "Prud'homme-Roquier House," Natchitoches Convention and Visitors Bureau, accessed September 17, 2017, https://www.natchitoches.com/listing/prud%E2%80%99homme-%E2%80%93-roquier-house.
[148] "Prudhomme-Roquier House," Cane River National Heritage Area, accessed September 17, 2017, https://www.nps.gov/nr/travel/caneriver/pru.htm.
[149] "Prud'homme-Roquier House," Natchitoches Convention and Visitors Bureau, accessed September 17, 2017, https://www.natchitoches.com/listing/prud%E2%80%99homme-%E2%80%93-roquier-house.
[150] "Prudhomme-Roquier House," Cane River National Heritage Area, accessed September 17, 2017, https://www.nps.gov/nr/travel/caneriver/pru.htm.

[151] Shreveport *Times*, April 9, 1916, p. 20.
[152] New Orleans *Times-Democrat*, March 30, 1891, p. 6.
[153] Shreveport *Times*, February 8, 1924, p. 10.
[154] "Don Theater," Louisiana Regional Folklife Program, accessed September 21, 2017, https://folklife.nsula.edu/civilwartocivilrights/05DonTheater.html.
[155] Shreveport *Times*, May 26, 1976, p. 29.
[156] Natchitoches *Times*, September 22, 1916, p. 1.
[157] "Tauzin-Wells House," Cane River National Heritage Area, accessed October 8, 2017, https://www.nps.gov/nr/travel/caneriver/tau.htm.
[158] "Tauzin-Wells House," Cane River National Heritage Area, accessed October 8, 2017, https://www.nps.gov/nr/travel/caneriver/tau.htm.
[159] Natchitoches *Times*, September 22, 1916, p. 1.
[160] Phoenix *Arizona Republic*, October 19, 1969, p. 123.
[161] Opelousas Daily World, January 12, 1971, p. 4.
[162] Bonnie Warren, "Living History," Louisiana Life Magazine, accessed October 8, 2017, http://www.myneworleans.com/Louisiana-Life/March-April-2010/Living-History/.
[163] Bonnie Warren, "Living History," Louisiana Life Magazine, accessed October 8, 2017, http://www.myneworleans.com/Louisiana-Life/March-April-2010/Living-History/.
[164] "Roselawn," Cane River National Heritage Area, accessed October 8, 2017, https://www.nps.gov/nr/travel/caneriver/ros.htm.
[165] Bonnie Warren, "Living History," Louisiana Life Magazine, accessed October 8, 2017, http://www.myneworleans.com/Louisiana-Life/March-April-2010/Living-History/.

CPSIA information can be obtained
at www.ICGtesting.com
Printed in the USA
LVHW040909221119
638065LV00002B/693/P

9 781706 526391